VINES TO MAKE IT ALL WORTH IT

Mia Fernandez

Contents:

To my mind,
Why have you forgiven me?

Stories and Poems

I'm a poet. I write in whispers only heard by the world. I'm a psychic of emotion. A scribe for every glimpse of feeling I observe. I catch the light in a person's gaze. I bottle sorrow bleeding from the heart. I write little. Each word carries more meaning by design. I tell stories in ten sentences. Shorter than a novel's prologue. Longer than an emotion is felt. Such a gift of quick pace does come with flaws. I write too quickly for myself. For a story allows such a length of appreciation, an honesty with complete understanding. Long chapters that humble my heavy words. My journaling of the mind is just a fraction of another's truth. But stories, ones of length and hardship, of promise and praise, of plot and careful planning, stories are what express the desires of the unspoken or shamed. But I am a poet. A diary for the otherwise forgotten moments in time. So, I will write lessons down as such. I will let you hold my words, and you may decide and define them.

For The Soil
Because the grass knew that the sun would come back.

Raised by Wolves

I once believed in flawed potential
covered myself in false essentials
relied too heavily on material gain
left spiritual desires unobtained
My body exhausted from the pain
of constant force of feet at search
for something brighter than the dirt
something bright like blood in snow
a wish on others for avenged sorrow

Rebuilding myself with shredded bone
the wolves come out to fetch me
drag me to the den called home
they lick me clean of envy
they scratch and tear pale skin like snow
claws seeping in skin to write
You're dead to me

Now I am anew
met in a reflection of blood I drew
still raw and exposed
dirty as a wolf's sliced bone
grasping life with new desire
hunting with possession for power
what was lost in myself
I'll no longer be confined from.
This time I won't be cleaned of shame

my former body a feast of remains
drowning in green insatiable hunger
the pack feeds off me, broken and sundered

It was once my fault
I denied who I was
tried to be greater than fate
refused the skin I was made of
I forced maturity through pain not age
Now my remorse and guilt mix with the rain,
I bury my old bones to stay dry of it.
yet the wolves let it mix with their pride

How could you poison me?

ivy necklace
draped like weeds
around my neck
thorns like beads
you cut my throat
ruby jewels that bled
an emerald shine
poisoned leaves

a false design
that ivy vine
that looks like herb
tastes like mine
from a garden I had
mint like my tea
you swelled my tongue
unable to breathe

now the vine chokes
i feel it prick
red rash that grows
undesirable itch
but you were beautiful once
you told me that too
pain wraps around me
i'm left poisoned like you

Two Trees

For the two trees we cut down from my backyard,
       who wore bugs and birds nest decor
       with branches swaying around the stars
       who danced along with cool summer breezes
       and offered shade to the grass on my lawn

I'm sorry
       that you did not get to rot in the soil you were
       planted in
       that you did not get to sag so low you broke
       my house
       that the air was hot and sticky when you both
       fell
       that all we left were your roots tangled
       beneath our ground

       for the two trees we cut down from the yard,
       I'm sorry
Forgive me for not hugging you before you left

Decomposing

What will the birds think when they see of your
demise?
       rotting carcass of a tree
        cut and robbed for a fire
Will they remember your glorious leaves?
       bright and golden
        breaking free
Will they mourn who you were last spring?
       sprouting new life
        shelter throughout and within
Or will they only see what could've been?
       old and ancient
        thick bark like skin

       I hope they see the rings on your stump
      the life you did live
the sanctuary you brought
       I hope they spot your roots still intact
      strong and withstanding
gripping under the grass
       And how you faced each day with pride
      touching the sky
limitlessly high

I wish the Earth had grown you legs
      when the lumberjack came,
        before the axe made you beg

Butterfly Net

I don't enjoy being tangled
in a net with flying incapable
It makes my mind unstable
burdens my heart with distress
leaving my spirit unrest
I cannot unwrap my thoughts
tried but failed to remove the knots
trapped in guilt I thought I forgot
cocooned myself in a mess I brought

I don't need solutions
words of improvement
No silent mockery
no more disillusions
I need gentle hands
a flower to lure me
a garden of sanctuary
a promise of maturity
rescue from resentment
I need quiet acceptance
tranquil gifts of honestly
help to find where my head went

I crave comfort
Please don't ask how I lost it
didn't mean to lose my soul
kept forgetting to watch it

Forgive me like a butterfly
treat me delicately
I wish for grace
renewal from release
Please offer me a place of peace
then lift my net to set me free

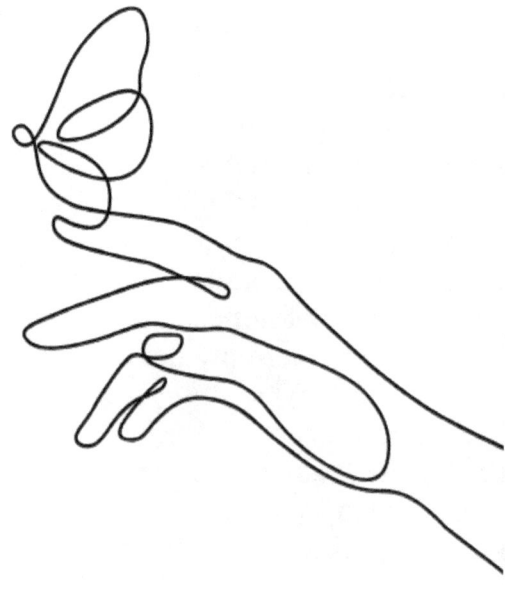

The Broken House Hums

Bird call cracks the still morning air. The leaves shift and breathe around their presence. It was Spring the last time I was here. Hot and sticky, sun glare in my eyes, I squint at the door and walk nearer. What is it about this house that keeps bringing me back to it? It's not mine, and not my parents. I'm not sure it's anyone's anymore. The door is torn down, and the roof is open, inviting the sky to join my return. Warm air saunters in beside me, embracing the house as it fills the empty rooms. And the wind I feel racing as it whistles to greet me, enters through the wooden cracks in the wall. Everything here still remembers my face; I try my best to visit and not be forgotten. I'm always welcomed in by the broken glass windows and bugs peeking out to witness my arrival. Is there anything prettier than this? Watching what's left of society as it crumbles. Slowly trickling back into Earth, it's home, where everything it was built with began from. The vines come back, twisting on the floor, beetles live in the kitchen, hiding where food was stored, and when the rain comes in through the ceiling it sags down the carpet and floor. And when I enter, I add to the decay, my shoes beat into the wood and leave mud stains. Now I'm a part of the collapse. And it's quiet, not insane. I don't fear the wild, it's soft like the moss and fog shrouding what remains. I'm grateful to these woods for the house it hides delivers me free rein. Of myself and of the Earth, of the small amount of peace I can sustain.

For The Sea
Because it washed me clean with love.

Four Years Ago: May 26th

I promised the ocean my spirit when I died
she told me she'd brush my hair with her current
that sand would untangle my curls
I'd be fed fish born from her stomach
oysters would dress me in their pearls
she'd lavish seaweed over my shoulders
drap me in her dripping scarves
cover my scars and mend my fractures
wrap me in a sea foam shine

Sea-light would pour from the moon that night
sprinkles spotting the water like glitter from the sky
I'd lay my body to rest in her tide
I'd give her my heart
pray she was kind

I tried to hand her my soul that day
and she did not accept it.
She said I must live with it first

Whale Fall

Beneath the blue
a whale fell
his mate died at sea
he followed her sound

They once moved together
swam beside the other
hummed as one
breached and bellowed

But now they sink
bodies sleeping, silencing howls
tonight they hit the bottom
deep beneath the ocean's power

It is quiet below here
in dark and shadowed waters
beneath the land's wake
silence owns this chasm

Tomorrow there will be a feast
beckoned by the whale fall
coral blooms around the grave
over the bodies, sea creatures sprawl

New life has formed
and the whales disappear

soon their mass is overtaken
eventually, the sea floor will clear

Waves Of My Hair

The sea sparks serpent's movement
        bare feet slithering among crushed shell
Footprints sink within wet sand
        washed back into place with each step

Wet curls surround my head
        wrapped around my neck like Medusa
Hair like snakes born from my head
        my hands working to calm them

My hair is hissing
        sand sprays against my skin
Wind spikes me with it to scrub me down
        the snakes move to twist and spin

I'm natural in all my glory
        as the sea pulls away my last shed
Born free and renewed by my rebirth
        wind tousles the swirls on my head

I let them be now
        a definition of me
Loose coils of serpents
        fresh scaled and sleek

Don't tame such a beast
        each curl earns its own keep

But won't turn you to stone or sand
    with acceptance they'll sleep

Love To My Ocean

Although I cannot tell you in person
I write letters of how I love you like the sea

Deep blue gaze of love from afar
a misty morning tranquility

broken by brilliant beams of white
the sky sends to sprint alongside our glee

We're racing with the flying fish!
Water splashing in delight at our flee

The seagulls laugh along with us
dolphins chase our running feet

Gliding with bliss and enlightenment
the seals squeak and join our odyssey

The sun has arrived!
The corals gleam bright

I love you like the fish
love the sea and it's might

So when you open my letters
let the beach bring you back to my life

Solace For Nature

Humanity is my biggest fear
so morbid we derive power from tears
scrap the blood from skin that's torn
seeping from our wounded foes
Can we create such monstrous war?
Then lose a battle the dead don't resolve
But smile in the face grief?
Laugh when one's failure completes
Pain so strong one fights themself
to earn their own life
one taken from them
If by their own hands their soul fly free
may God send rest to such minds that flee

We're too versatile
skin like rubber
with eyes of glass
a voice that stutters
Hands that claw and rip
and tear
Feet that can kick and run
yet fail
I forget myself
What a terrible creation
one that celebrates such similar spaces
How can I cherish the likes of nature?
Mother Earth always sending her hatred

She sends a flood to drown our fighting
cracks her skin to crumble our biting
shakes the air to stir the clouds
swallows her sky
strikes fire to the ground

Yet we both still strive
hurting ourselves
hurting each other
Against all terrors
still surviving amongst the horrors
Laughing while the clouds above cry
Birds that sing over bombs that fly
Above all the chaos
and echoing screams and lies

Will you forgive my preference of opposition
The likes of one terror over my own instinctions?
For I have grown too close to humanity's jagged
edges
have scars to prove how barbaric their cut is
But her, Mother Nature, I have not known enough to
fear yet
her wind is soft when tucking my hair back
she glows my eyes with light like beautiful reflections
her flowers grow just to see what dwells above them
Such innocence she has, yet she masks her danger
I know her capabilities
she's as strong as our hate is

But I love her, our Earth,
she desires empathy
and she forgives herself
that's more than society has allowed me

And For The Sky
Because the birds never forget to wake me.

A Bird's Back

The gift of flight
        Magic of wings
                Whispering wind
                        Air that sings
A bird's back
        Strength to fly free
                Return of morning light
                        Come and whistle with me
Watch the birds soar
        They race to dazzle
                A sky full of others
                        Shadows moving together
Glide back to Earth
        Bring with you warm breeze
                Bathe in cool water
                        Wash beneath the trees
Bask in the clouds
        Embrace the unknown
                Carry pride in each stroke
                        Drop feathers as you go
Upon a bird's back
        Aspirations guide you home
                With hope that fuels desire
                        A heart full of warm song

Find Me A Blue Sky

Find me a blue sky
I'll love her,
Find me the scripture
she taught better than others,
give me a sky vibrating with color
Clouds that swirl and sway with one another.
Our great blanket of cover
rising each day to grant us comfort,
I weep in her sink of stars at night
I laugh with her sunshine filling my cup

Oh, how colorful
each season may change
bring new shades of leaves and more rain
But the sky,
how blue she remains
hums the rhythm of my heartbeat
a joyous song the birds sing.
She grants me gorgeous words,
I spread her gifts of peace
and I praise the sky,
its glory washes my hands and feet

She wakes me each day
with new delight that drives
my stories and creation

Lights my mind with Holy Fire,
and steam drifts up from within
fills where my thoughts form
new growth dances a display of gratitude
and the Earth rebuilds, untorn

And the Sun Came Back

God created the light
And He saw that the light was good

What was it that made it good?
That it was His?
A first creation
fulfilling its will
That it was quiet?
With nothing to disobey
nothing to whisper with
no way for it to decay
That it was beautiful?
Enabling the eyes
unleashing the Earth
freeing the sky
That it divided the darkness?
And cleared the fog
defeated the veil
pulled the cloth

No,
He loved it because it created too
began the first day
a day built of truth
It was the glorious beginning
creation from creation

the first breath of life
humanity's inspiration

So He let the light be
And the light was good

Only Ones Who Know

There is a feeling buried here
I felt it long before you said,
   You hid it far above the sky
   but stars rarely silence sentiments

The cosmos told me all your secrets
soft confessions with kind intent
Comets that raced to hush my worry
   craters convincing my head to rest

At night the air is stirring,
The sun has taken its bow
   Constellations come out to clap for her
   My dreams come from their sound

Among the stars you held my hand
I smiled at you then as I do,
   We traced ourselves into the dust
   That's when I figured you knew

That before the sun would rise again
We'd orbit towards the truth
   You'd place your palms on astral rock
   only then, would you see
     I would've given you the moon too

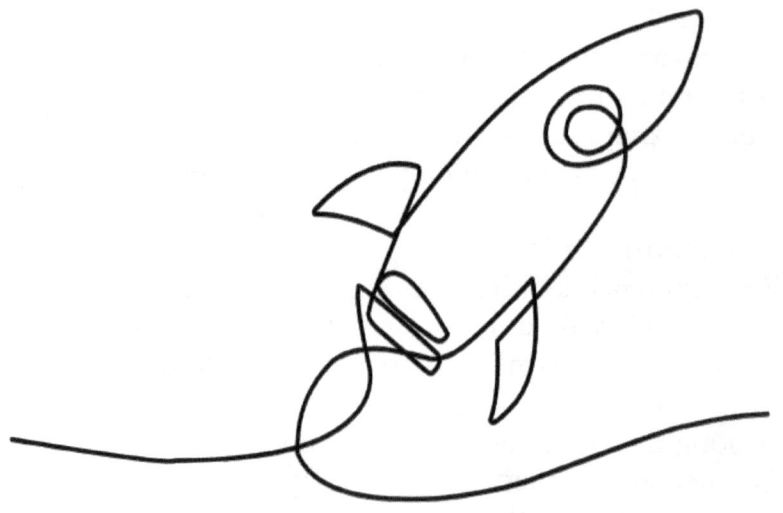

ACKNOWLEDGEMENTS
To God and his creation. To the birds who live in the tree by my window. To the memories that made this which I pray I don't forget. To the kids in 1313, thank you for all the laughs.

Mia Fernandez has grown and lost throughout her life as the seasons do. She finished Vines To Make It All Worth It in the Spring of 2025 before her high school graduation at Charles J. Colgan Sr. High School. There she was a part of the Center of Fine and Preforming Arts Creative Writing program where she created and grew her poetic voice with the help of some of the funniest people she'll ever know. She has published pieces in the school's literary journal, Siren. She likes how grass feels on bare feet and hates when bugs get caught in her hair. She wishes she liked reading more.